# See My Feathered Fingers

**Elaine Barker**

# See My Feathered Fingers

## Acknowledgements

Some of the poems in this collection have been previously published
in the following journals, newspapers and anthologies:
*Bimblebox 153 Birds, Blue Giraffe, Collecting Writers, Eureka Street,*
the Friendly Street Poets anthologies, *In Daily, Poems in Perspex,
Poetry Monash, Studio, Tamba, That Which My Eyes See, The Canberra
Times, The Heart of Port Adelaide, The Mozzie, The Shanghai Literary
Review, Through the Tunnel, Westerly, Wild, Women's Work*;
and also in my previous collections:
*The Windmill's Song, The Day Lit by Memory*
and *High Heels & Tartan Slippers.*

For my family and all my friends and fellow poets.

With special thanks to Victoria Barker and Jan Owen
for their editorial assistance.

*See My Feathered Fingers*
ISBN 978 1 76041 754 3
Copyright © Elaine Barker 2019
Cover: Miriam Barker-Lanzi
Author photo: Lisa Lanzi

First published 2019 by
**Ginninderra Press**
PO Box 3461 Port Adelaide 5015
www.ginninderrapress.com.au

# Contents

| | |
|---|---|
| These Small Things | 9 |
| **I The Day Is Heavy With Sunlight** | **11** |
| Crushed Berries | 13 |
| Certainty | 14 |
| On the Footpath | 15 |
| Summer Secrets | 16 |
| Lizard | 17 |
| In Grandmother's Garden | 18 |
| The Cedars | 19 |
| Autumn | 20 |
| Toy Boys | 21 |
| Walking Away | 22 |
| Child and Dog | 23 |
| Feathering the Nest | 24 |
| The Stubble Quail | 25 |
| The Brass Plaque | 26 |
| Urban Pastoral | 27 |
| The Lady and the Bees | 28 |
| Burning | 29 |
| A Confusion of Wings | 30 |
| Fire of Australia | 31 |
| Acquisitions | 32 |
| **II The Rhythm of the House** | **33** |
| The Ansonia Clock | 35 |
| Jelly Mould | 36 |
| Flycatcher | 37 |
| The Yoke | 38 |
| Mixed Media | 39 |
| Relics | 40 |

| | |
|---|---|
| The Fan | 42 |
| The Cape | 43 |
| Frederick Franklin's Photograph | 44 |
| Worn With Pride | 45 |
| The Fancy Hat | 46 |
| Nets | 47 |
| The Brooch | 48 |
| A Brass Button | 49 |
| The Fixer | 50 |
| Smoke Rings | 51 |
| The Fox Fur | 52 |
| Small Sounds In the Night | 53 |
| Summer Morning | 54 |
| For Moses | 55 |
| Blue Crystal Beads | 56 |
| The Wedding Ring | 57 |
| A Snatch of Memory | 58 |
| Glass | 59 |
| Baby and Shawl | 60 |
| Patchwork Blanket | 61 |
| See My Feathered Fingers | 62 |
| Scar | 63 |
| Cleaning Out the House | 64 |
| The Porcelain Bowls | 65 |
| Connections | 66 |
| **III That Far Landscape** | **67** |
| Baggage | 69 |
| Birch Broom | 70 |
| The Tablet | 71 |
| Quipu | 72 |
| Featherwork | 73 |

| | |
|---|---:|
| The Sound of Jade Earrings | 74 |
| Sepik Mask | 75 |
| Tang Figurine | 76 |
| Nails | 77 |
| The Bronze Hand | 78 |
| The Turban | 79 |
| In Afghanistan | 80 |
| In the Ukraine | 81 |
| Field Flowers | 81 |
| The Floating Islands | 82 |
| The Finger | 83 |
| The Citadel | 84 |
| Bamboo | 85 |
| Riding the Ocean | 86 |
| Caught In the Weather | 87 |
| Burial of St Catherine of Alexandria | 88 |
| The Merry Cemetery | 89 |

# These Small Things

Here between the pages of a book, a tiny feather
I picked up while walking years ago. A puff of grey down,
it expands at one end into a minute fan of yellow and red.
And as I finger it now I'm reminded of leaves
and flowers and stones and small creatures –
mere fragments of the world that enfolds us.
I'm conscious of their charm and fragility.
And where we live small objects surround us –
those companionable pieces, the bric-a-brac,
the pots and pans of life, the commonplace.
Rather than the greater event these are most often recalled,
along with the everyday happenings that shape our lives.
Consider actions as simple and small as a touch,
a smile, a gesture only later understood,
fleeting moments of clarity
and sounds and tastes and smells and small certainties,
interactions with people never seen again.
We share images of places known
and things from other times and other lands,
such images and voices tell us who we are.
It's the montage of memories and fragments that endures,
these gathering and adjusting and drawing energy
to form a space for a lifetime of ideas.
These small things exist within us and in the end
will fit together one final time when we will almost understand.

# 1

# The Day Is Heavy With Sunlight

# Crushed Berries

When the sun's a fiery disk hanging
low on the horizon
its light streams out across the park
to this row of peppertrees,
glinting through the lacy foliage,
and in an illusion turns
the edges of the leaves
silver or crystal rather than gold.

The peppertree berries crushed in your hand
then smell sweet and sharp and hot.

In that thin space of time
in early evening the trees appear
to muster their branches
to trap the molten sunball,
embracing it fleetingly
before it drops from sight.

# Certainty

for Denis

If I had told you
about the spiderweb
that spanned the distance
between two small branches
on the prunus tree
I'd come upon that cold morning
on the path across the garden
and if I'd spoken of its spare mystery
the threads strung from its bridge line
each silk strand spun with dewdrops
each glistening sharp and fine,
that web would have drawn you in
and you would have marvelled
at its mathematical precision
its clarity of design
and would have pictured it
like an unspoken whisper
and carried it with you
as I have done.

# On the Footpath

I love the plump and particular
pattern of your days,
your quiet pecking
and unpicking of the path.
I love your bob-bob bebopping
dappled-brown meandering.

Odd, that I've never seen you young
or ailing. And I can safely say
I've never seen a sparrow fall.
I wonder where you go to die.

Rather, I remember you
when not in flight
but as a celebration of sparrows
feather-blown at my feet.
As you take wing my spirits lift;
in each of you, an elemental truth.

I love the way you casually flit
in and out of life;
the way that you create
a simple happening in the street.

## Summer Secrets

Midmorning finds me in the shed,
tools on the bench, the smell of turps,
cocooned in the safety of silence.
But not as I think alone, for something
easing along the border of things
whispers me from the shadow's edge.
A snake is hugging the shed
where wall meets floor, its progress
insistent yet silken as a caress
or like a ripple on the river bank
and that same colour, the colour of mud.
As if following a dream
when my shocked eyes open into night
I watch long after the shape has gone.
But tell no one, recall not awe nor fear,
only the mystery of movement drawn out,
and that intrusion into workaday space,
odds and ends crowding the concrete floor,
those wood shavings scattered about.

## Lizard

The lizard who nicks across
my cottage garden is back again.
It's made camp somewhere nearby
and now prowls through lush flower beds
to lie in wait for beetles and insects,
letting slip that fiendish blue tongue.

Delicately negotiating obstacles in the way
it's heading off to a stand of gums
where you can follow its progress
in the slight rustle of fallen bark.
And here it becomes one with shades
of ochre and sand and rust.
Rearranging the bark imperceptibly
it connects with the earth, with the land
and soon it's returning, trailing noiselessly
beneath red roses and native flannel flowers.

# In Grandmother's Garden

Then death and dolls and darkness edged her life,
the maze of portraits in passageways
by night, the dark made strange with tinsel light.
Day smocked the garden with shadows, with flowers,
ribbons of content in the sound of a dove.
Her hours were spent noiselessly.
She, the sensual collector of red berries,
lone observer of leaves burning,
the sometime protector of a doll.
The bright sorrow of a pretended grave
would please her, the whiteness of lilies.
Unattended now she roams her garden,
seeks her pattern in pathways, the perfume
of burning leaves still lingering in a dove's call.

# The Cedars

The Cedars is the name of the home of the artist Hans Heysen

Though wintry the light in the garden
is as bright as first love.
It illuminates leafless branches
where firepoints of dripping colour
are thrown in circles of radiance
as the sun drops and dies.
Now the crickets have come out
and birds are getting ready for night
and somewhere, self-satisfied,
a kookaburra lets go a laugh.
Then all is still.
Dusk has made stars of the jonquils,
their pale perfume in the air.
Trees are falling into their shadows
as a monotone spreads over the place
and the lighter tones of a watercolour
have faded to a sober oil.
A gravel path hurries towards
the solid comfort of the house.

## Autumn

Along the street a stiff wind
has sent leaves slanting, yellowing down.
The trees are left sculptural and bent

and on the ground the leaves settle,
subside, lie fallow a while,
tinder dry and resting.

Today a slight breeze is lifting them
and each leaf ruffles, ripples, fidgets, flutters
until, drawn together

they form a cavalcade on the path
like a gaggle of youngsters, hit and run,
unable to keep still.

All at once a single leaf careers
helter-skelter out in front of the pack.
You can almost hear it laugh

as it skitters along and it sets you thinking
of those children who are always in the lead
as if aware already of their destiny.

## Toy Boys

The gnomes I chose are stop-at-homes.
This spot in my garden is the place
they gaudily claim. Though gnomes
do roam – you hear of them
disappearing months at a time.
They send cards from wherever
they've been, only to reappear
one morning tight-lipped, benign.

Yet no such trivial travel
would ever interest my gnomes.
Like a squat of fancy birds
they parade, preen, step out
untrammelled from the ferns.
Accepting a terracotta life
they raise red-hatted heads,
might grumble at unseasonal rains.

# Walking Away

There's a heady smell of damp earth.
It's a winter's day and I'm watching
poppies flash their carnival colours
and dance a tango in the wind
when all at once a magpie jerks its body
across the path and into a garden bed.

My dog is ranging round the park.
He sees the bird then backs away,
cocks his head and moves on,
turning a blameless face to mine.
I can't think what to do.
I fix his lead. As we race the lap
of yellow leaves toward the gate
a boast of boys with idle eyes
and heavy boots
comes clattering into the park.
I choose not to think, choose
to turn away from the creature
with the broken body, the limping wing.

Escapees on the run, we bolt headlong
down the living street.
My woolly-haired dog is in command.
His mouth is open, laughing.
We are alive, alive. And all at once
I'm laughing as I follow him.

# Child and Dog

The day is heavy with sunlight.
There's a fiery haze in the empty street.
All is quiet until a dog starts up.
The girl had wanted to stroke
the smooth warmth of its coat
but fear has diminished her
turning her into a folk tale figure.
She is lost, alone in the wild place
she knows from her storybooks.
She's afraid of the dog's heavy face,
the prick of its ears,
the set of its jaw,
the sudden flash of teeth.

Her pale legs are spread wide,
her feet locked into the stippled grass.
Her ponytail has ceased its bobbing,
lying quiet on her back.
Unprotected by the skimpy fabric
of her dress, her arms are weapons
ready to strike out.

Years later when she brings to mind
that dog day in summer she remembers
heat hanging like a veil over the street
and the animal's earthy smell,
the fleshy muzzle
and the insistent wolfish growl.

# Feathering the Nest

It seems nothing is sacred.
On the lawn, a drift of pale feathers
is all that remains of my cat's encounter
with one of their kind.
It carpets the meeting-place
for the pigeon's gentle protest
and as they circle the scene,
passing lightly by,
fellow pigeons close in.
Anarchic, knowing,
they are foragers, laying claim
to those relics remaining,
carrying feathers away to nearby trees,
pickpocketing memories.

# The Stubble Quail

I very nearly missed you
hunkered down there in a nest
hidden beneath a stunted bush
where only dry grasses were stirring
and I could almost believe
you were feathered insignificantly
until your modest colours
of tawny chestnut brown
were suddenly revealed
when at that moment the sun
burst through an overcast sky
to shine light on your homespun charm.

# The Brass Plaque

The seat is like any other in the park.
With its rustic supports and apt shade of green
it merges with the native trees
along with a few exotics, no more.
This seat bears a plaque and one chosen
by a family – Aleksander, Magnus, Lesley –
who named it 'Daddy's Bench' to honour
the man who so often rested here.
His name suggests his heritage
so that, if he heard wind sough through this pine
and took in the heady aroma
or stepped over pine needles on the grass
and felt them crush beneath his feet
it's possible he thought back to the homeland.
Today some Indian children are hard at cricket,
a couple huddle on a tartan rug,
a woman tries to restrain her kelpie
who is tangling with some magpies
having a natter nearby.
You make your way across the park, turn,
look back, and in that instant
the seat takes on a new dimension, it becomes
all-encompassing. More than a prop, a stay,
it accommodates a sense of history.
You see people from colonial days
stepping out the shape of the pathways,
you think of permanence and stability.

# Urban Pastoral

Hyde Park, Sydney

Like birds of prey, pigeons have descended
on a figure on the park bench.
It seems they've turned rogue
and heads intent, they are scrambling
around the man's upturned face.
Their outspread wings enmesh, rising
and falling, fanning out
to cover his tattered beanie
and the shoulders of his coat.
Softly sinister, they bill and coo
in vagrant shades of pearly grey.
As you come closer it's clear at once
that the birds are merely peckish
and are closing in on cupped hands,
hands that are spread out
and bountied with crumbs.
Other birds keep to the bright edges
of the park – a squabble of seagulls
dividing a crust, sparrows rallying,
while a single ibis, elegant as a queen,
steps out regally across the grass
in no need of charity and content to forage alone.

# The Lady and the Bees

It was a young woman in white overalls,
a hat with a fitted veil,
and with bare hands
who appeared at my door that morning
all those years ago.
From a safe distance I pointed
to the marauders who had seized
and taken control of our garden
where a glistening cone of bees,
a seething black and yellow mass,
nestled in celebration about their queen,
a sting at the heart of their high-pitched whine.
Warned to stay inside
I did not observe her expertise,
but she soon made a beeline for her van,
the swarm boxed on a pole across one shoulder
while a scatter of bees, hovering,
formed an escort around her.
Back at my door, she's free of the veil
and when I query her occupation
no honeyed words, just a wry toss of the head.
*The things I do for my husband*,
she simply said, and what struck me
was her freckled smile,
the flawless skin on each hand,
the sun-coloured hair, amber eyes,
the patch of pollen on her chin.

# Burning

Those days with a bittersweet burning
the sky and sea and sand became their world,
the beach a great void taking them in.
The weight of the sun soothed their limbs
as they lazed in the shallows,
splashes of laughter around them,
shrieks of little kids running free,
the sniping of seagulls,
ceaseless waves embracing the shore.
Lounging in the water's velvet warmth,
they'd swap stories and half-truths
dare each other to stare at the sun.
They collected shells and cuttlefish,
strands of seaweed with its dark sweaty smell.
They spent time patterning a sandcastle
until tired of the game they smashed
it down, trampling the remnants into the ground.
A treat, to see a windblown umbrella
cartwheeling along the beach
while a band of boys like warriors
after prey set off in pursuit.
The tide tongued in to fill their pool
and on their bellies in the shallows again
they'd lie daydreaming, sorting out possibilities.
In the backseat on the way home
they pressed close, leg to leg, thigh to thigh,
bodies itching with salt, growing breasts taut.
At night they'd lie awake, skin silky
with oil and burning, at one with the sun.

# A Confusion of Wings

There's a confusion, an unpacking of wings:
wings that are gossamer, iridescent and strong.
It's as if black-edged panels of orange and cream
like segments from a stained glass window
have all at once taken to the air.
As the great mass surges into the sky's vault
some butterflies are already sloughing off.
What would you expect?
They are drifting, withering like spent flowers,
falling further than any flower could fall.
And yet the rest press south and on,
to become mere specks in the firmament,
the sun glancing off millions of sparkling wings,
on the steady sweep of their journey, its certainty.
An impulse keeps them moving,
sometimes riding the thermals,
until over central Mexico they coast,
they glide, their goal at hand,
and tentatively hovering,
they slowly waft their way to earth.
Their six stick legs stretch, brace and claw,
their interlaced wings shimmering,
as the spicy foliage of the Oyamel fir
beds them down, takes them in.

# Fire of Australia

Fire of Australia, the name given to the world's finest uncut opal, is in the collection of the South Australian Museum

Among those roaming people, first in the land,
many found meaning in opal.
Some believed it was flung from the sky
in lighting strikes, compressed flame,
the scorched crimsons and corals
and watery flashes of blue and green
spilling out to merge and swirl
and dance across the rock's pale surface.

In the museum we learn that silica and water
once filled cracks and crevices in the earth
and then, over time, the spaces turned lustrous,
glimmering and opaline.

And yet I warm to the view that opal
was a gift from above and wonder
at the way the colours fuse and coalesce,
while the pearly haze caught in this stone
is seen in the mists of early morning,
mists that link country and sky.

# Acquisitions

Rye, England

Tumbled by currents, trashed by the ocean,
pebbles like these misted in sea spray
layer the beach in their millions
and stumbling over the shingles,
revelling in their numbers,
I souvenired those that caught my eye.
Dislodged from ancient cliffs,
plucked up, pulled and pummelled,
the stones are worn away
and fashioned into their sweeping lines
by the sea's to and fro.

Some are long and lean, some full-bellied,
some smooth as a woman's breast,
while one carries within its bulk
a tiny pebble as snug as any embryo.
And the markings they display are singular,
some mottled like granite
or splashed in streaks and shadows,
a few patterned delicately as a sparrow's egg.

I've transported my takings to the Antipodes
where, weight massed on a copper tray,
they recline in light bright colours –
slate grey, sepia and ginger, brown and fawn
and one, pure poetry, of a startling white.

# II

# The Rhythm of the House

## The Ansonia Clock

Its place is on my kitchen shelf.
My clock surveys me, directs my days,
its ways unchanging.

A wooden fretwork forms a topknot
above the commanding face
where Roman numerals mark the hours.

Below, the pendulum, a silver disk,
swings regularly back and forth,
that sound unfailing.

Best of all, the glass door carries
a catching design of bamboo fronds
and a tracery of flowers.

I've known my clock for over sixty years.
It relies on frequent winding
and even when I pass on the task

the steady beat will measure time long
after I am gone, that simple sound
the mainstay of a home.

## Jelly Mould

There's verve and a mellow warmth
in the copper that forms this mould.
See how light catches each curve
of its fluted sides and again
at the base where a floral design shapes
the jelly that, with a plop, comes slithering out.

Consider Harriet the young kitchen hand.
Under Cook's direction she'll hold the mould
in hot water but only long enough
for the glistening shape to slip away
and, if she's lucky, it will sit
precisely in the centre of the crystal serving dish.

It would be her wish to taste the jelly
or at least to see it grace the banquet table,
but that handsome young waiter Emanuel
will carry it in. He'll put it down
and later he'll take her arm and show her
the grandeur of the setting under candlelight.

## Flycatcher

Form follows function and reaching high
this glass dome is topped by a neat glass stopper.
At the base three sturdy feet lend stability.
You may wonder at the configuration:
the way the dome's base turns up, then in
to provide a continuous inner rim.
Here beer was placed to entice
blowflies and other insects to slip inside.
And so the teeming mass was trapped.
On kitchen shelf or dining room dresser
in every colonial house or homestead
the flycatcher admirably fulfilled its function.

Today a soapy wash, a rinse and polish
has given the piece a jaunty lustre.
Despite its humble past it has outlasted
other less sturdy glass.
My guests can never guess its use,
its age or worth. I let it stand
beside a copper jelly mould,
as a handsome curio on my side table.

## The Yoke

How many necks has this yoke pressed?
And how many pails of fresh warm milk
have swung splashing from its arms?
Or weighty containers of grain?

Skilled hands shaped this rustic piece
with an adze, the graceful form drawn from oak.
It was fashioned to hug the shoulders
but the years too have rounded out
the already carefully crafted edges.

My old clock ticks on across the room
but the yoke is at ease, at home.
It's thrown off an inbuilt image
of servitude. Its labouring days are done.

## Mixed Media

after Rosalie Gascoigne's assemblage *Enamel ware*, 1976

Precisely aligned, three crates form
both shelving and picture frame
for an accumulation of enamel ware.
These pieces fit nicely together,
and all are from the same era.
To hand, a sieve or colander,
pannikins, teapot, a jug for pouring
and pie plates, pan and bowl,
each of them licked round with rust,
scraped right out or eaten through.
You've put a finger on their homely role.
You've fossicked about, done the tip,
brought them all together
and even then you've thought
to screw them down so they won't be
nicked or pinched or borrowed.
You've taken us back to earlier times,
to the smell of a woodstove,
the noise of a dripping tap,
the everyday sound of splashing milk
or a ticking clock.
Out in the yard the crows scare,
make ready to take flight and then
mooch darkly off across the sky.

# Relics

Collection of the Hyde Park Barracks Museum, Sydney

From beneath the floorboards, between the walls,
from ceilings or the fetid corners
thousands of artefacts have been recovered,
this detritus giving voice to the soldiers,
the convict men and women and the outcasts
who at different times made this building home.

Everyday objects are glass-cased here –
a spoon, a fork and a bone-handled knife,
a broken cup, a small green bottle,
a spill of blue and white china.
There are fragments of food –
animal bones, peach stones,
a handful of peanut shells
and now, playing cards, old coins,
glass shards and tarnished buttons,
tangled snippets and lengths of string.

Here are more personal things
and women bend in to examine a lice comb,
a clay pipe, hairpins, part of a fan.
Next, a child's tooth, possibly a keepsake,
mislaid or lost or swept out of sight.
And a scattering of clothing, remnants of cloth,
moth-eaten shreds of cotton and wool.

There's a rat's nest here and it's plain
that she'd laid claim to anything at hand –
wisps of lace, bits of ribbon, knots of hair,
and all kinds of oddments she'd salvaged
to shore up the lair that's on display.
Her skeleton lies close by
and with it the remains of her litter –
mere scraps of existence, like crumpled stones.
This rat too is part in the story.
She also set out on a journey,
made landfall and ventured ashore.
In the end she crept into a dark corner
to become a relic and part of the exhibition.

Here's a handwritten letter torn in half.
In the broken hope it could be forgotten,
did someone hide it out of sight?

After all these years the personal becomes public.
Time telescopes, as assessed and sorted,
named and numbered, these found pieces
find their own place under glass.
They tug at our thoughts, connect
with our lives, draw us into the past.

This is the exhibit that made me smile –
a silver coin has been knotted into a corner
of a faded cotton handkerchief.
I used to carry money like that
when, a lifetime ago, I walked to school.

# The Fan

Collection of the National Gallery of Victoria, feathered fan, c.1880

Her laugh was too loud,
her dress too red
and the fan she carried
sparked whispers around the room.
It was said a Chinese man
had worked the fine ivory handle
and the silken tassel and cord,
but it was the cockatoo feathers
lurid in scarlet and black,
that caught the eye.
The older ladies turned away.
The young ones clustered close,
and the gentlemen too,
to learn of her travels,
to wonder at her accent
and marvel at the words she used.
She set her head
on one side like a bird
while the lazy fan wafted
sulkily back and forth, to and fro.
I stood close to see
her glittering fingers
as she dallied with the fan
on that steamy evening
in Palmerston, here in the far north.

# The Cape

Collection of the National Gallery of Victoria, platypus pelt fur, c.1890

She would have it. She must have it.
He agreed the cape was handsome
and saw how her face opened and shone.
Strange how the fur matched her own hair,
the glistening sheen fading to silver, to grey.
From memory he reckoned it wombat skin.
But no. *Stitched together from the platypus, sir.*
*And from over the water – Van Diemen's Land.*
Once more, he braced against the wind's weight,
the crosshatched rain, the learning and unlearning,
the flow of time and the ways of men.

*This cape is very unique and if I may say, sir,*
*it suits her ladyship very fine.*
Running his hands through the depth of the pelt
he breathed in a fragrance, something like honey.
He saw how the cape sat snug at her throat,
encircled her body, showing to advantage
the sleeves of her fashionable gown.
She must have it. She would have it.
Pride pulled his wallet from out of his pocket.

He had the furrier summon his carriage
where he rested his head at last on her shoulder,
sharing with her this mysterious fur.
Content, he eased back in his seat
accepted the warm face of the day,
took pleasure in the comfort, the smell of leather,
and the clip-clop of Molly and Daisy
as they rattled apace along Collins Street.

# Frederick Franklin's Photograph

The photographer has positioned
his hunting party clustered round their Chrysler
in front of a tidy limestone house.
The men are well equipped against the cold
with hats and boots and overcoats.
Suits are crumpled and second-best
yet good enough for a hunting trip.
There's a claim to training and expertise
in the precise slope of their rifles;
in South Africa perhaps, against the Boer.
Gold watch chains dangle grandly
across the surfeit of each portly chest.
There's a formal stamp on the picture's reverse
with faded names in copperplate: Henry and Edward,
Leonard and Albert, Harold and Jack.
You can catch their jokes, the tone of the laughter,
the facile songs and the drinking after.

In the background, a cottage garden
with a gravel path and a picket fence
and much further on,
paddocks flagged with unruly gums.
This is the hunting ground
of the earliest people in the land
and finding themselves in focus,
they slipped away beyond this frame.
They timed the seasons and marked the skies,
passed lightly over these sepia plains.

# Worn With Pride

Collection of the South Australian Maritime Museum

In a cabinet there's an old-world bicorn hat
of black velour with an upturned brim,
eight silver tassels on either side,
a ribbon band and rosette completing the trim.
Decked in this ceremonial finery
the Inspector-General of the Royal Navy
would sweep on board, his eyes alert,
his feet caught in a rolling gait,
the stamp of a man at sea.

On the lower shelf there's a neat tin case
precisely designed to contain that hat.
So, imagine if you can the scene:
following in the great man's steps,
a sailor-suited blue-eyed British lad.
His duty – to carry the empty tin.
Already he's planning to go to sea,
to share in his nation's power
and quite possibly in its infamy.

# The Fancy Hat

after Roxanne Petrick's soft sculpture, one of the series *Every face has a story, every story has a face: Kulila!* 2016

Round Alice Springs nine women sat down
to sew and chat and share their yarns.
While they stitched their country into the story
they shared their tea and tucker too.
Linked by their lives and thoughts and expertise
they created soft sculptures of wool and cloth,
welcoming figures in this gallery space.
They wrapped stick bodies with patterns of their choice,
then each woman crafted an individual face.
*Kulila!* Listen. *Every face has a story,
every story has a face.* And Roxanne,
I admire your head with its neat bright stitching,
the emu feathers that form the hair
and most of all, the fancy hat
in colours of black and yellow and red.
Beneath the hat you've embroidered
a duplicate face with a different role.
We all have a particular tale to tell
about the person we once were.
Or could have been. Or wished to be.
This hidden face poses a mystery,
something not quite known or understood.
There's a stillness that carries the weight
and shape of what you might call hope.

# Nets

Collection of the South Australian Museum

There's grace in these nets
and the natural fall of them
and power in their simplicity.
Here the black man's lore
and storied dance live on
through the mesh,
the springy interlace
of sedge and grass and reed;
so that in this display
nets worked to capture
game or fish or bird
today reach out
to snare our thoughts
with an airy spread,
buoyant and assured.

# The Brooch

They'd handed him the letter that day,
told him the words he had to say.
He grabbed his bike and set off
into the blazing white of the runaway street,
rows of jacarandas leading him on,
their violet blue blossoms
falling like shadows round every tree.
He found the house, a bungalow,
propped his bike at the veranda's edge,
couldn't remember what he had to say,
presented the buff-coloured envelope instead
and rode off into the ache of the day,
flying dust his enemy in the stony street.
He thought back to the woman with her apron on,
the golden brooch pinned to her chest
with letters that spelt *mother*,
and how she'd accepted the letter and knew,
and the old man beside her too.
They had both said *thank you*
and then closed the door
so they could mourn alone
before the whole street knew, and the town.

## A Brass Button

While you were complaining about the waste
of time and money in the search
for human remains on the plains of northern France
and that, since so many years had passed,
the soldiers should be left to lie in the soil at peace

I'd been reading about the discovery of a skeleton
and a brass button engraved with a map of Australia
and that, if the man could be identified,
and buried with our rituals of grief and celebration,
his family could find their peace at last.

## The Fixer

My dad could put anything together –
a book respined, its pages realigned,
a toy, a game, a leather bag,
a flowerpot from the shed.
Rag in hand he'd squeeze a stream
of Tarzan's Grip and that enticing smell
was half the fun, but better still,
the picture on the tube:
Tarzan wrestling with a beast,
his chest and arms stripped bare,
one thigh exposed below a tiny loincloth.
Broken china was my father's speciality.
Jagged, jigsawed fragments only served
to spur him on – a teapot spout,
a jug, a willow pattern plate – each piece
matched, attached and tortuously made whole.
I'm standing here examining a vase
with cracks outlined in seeping glue,
discoloured now for sixty years.
I know I ought to throw it out and yet
it's hard to disregard his hold on things.

# Smoke Rings

My father always rolled his own.
First, I'd help tease out the tobacco strands,
taking in their tawny smell,
and he'd select a paper from the case.
He rolled it all together and then
he taught me to light a match,
to hold it close and still while he lit up.
As he inhaled, enthralled I'd wait to see
his mouth round out to form a perfect O.
Then breath-taking, a smoky ring rose high
into the air to hover and float in space
and together we would watch as slowly
the shape would simply disintegrate.
Much later my dad gave up the habit
and instead, he nibbled little bits of ginger
stored in his wartime tobacco tin.
Time came when he worked it out
or perhaps he had been warned –
blowing smoke rings was a dying art.

# The Fox Fur

It's a bit of history, no less.
We're all dressed up for a trip to town,
my grandmother, my brother and me,
and a street photographer has snapped us.
Was it his plan or serendipity
that our three left legs are stepping out as one?
My brother's eyes focus on the cameraman,
waiting for the tripod camera to flash.
In a pale coat and matching hat
I'm sight-seeing in the city for the very first time.
Our grandmother escorts us,
her energy constrained by her corset
and her costume's tight skirt.
She's wearing a feathered hat,
her leather gloves of course.
A crocheted bag is looped over her right wrist.
Yet this scene is held in my memory
for one thing only: the fox fur
creeping over my grandmother's shoulder.
I was permitted to open the box, to lift out the fur
and to savour its silky warm smell.
But what I remember best is how,
to fix it in place, I'd make the foxy teeth snap
fast over the bushy black tail.
Then I'd drape the fur fashionably
over my grandmother's chest.

# Small Sounds In the Night

I used to know the reason for those small sounds
that worry and make you anxious in the dark.
My grandmother's maid told me the story.
People came in at night, she said,
and rearranged the furniture in the house.
She sensed my doubt, said it was a secret,
a secret she could only share with me.
When I was eight I decided to surprise the intruders
but the night closed in, caught me in its grasp,
and creeping fear trapped me in my bed.
My comfort was the honeysuckle-scented breeze
that wafted through my window,
and sent the lace-edged curtains flaring out.
Mornings, Dolly was always up and dressed
and when I caught her eye she'd nod and wink
so I knew she'd set things right again.
By day, my grandfather's smoking room still carried
the aroma of his evening cigar.
I checked the position of each leather chair,
the tall bookshelves and the shiny smoking stand.
I was unsure about the sweeping roll-top desk.
Holidays over, I went home again
and those events quite slipped my mind.
Decades later and half asleep I heard a noise
and in an instant that memory returned to me.
I sat up. I sat up and I laughed out loud.
Dolly, it's unlikely you remembered me,
but I think of you, even if only occasionally.

# Summer Morning

after Hans Heysen's painting *Sewing*, 1913

This spot is fine for sewing,
a breeze touching the curtains
as the summer morning wafts in.
The woman is bending over work
at her New Home sewing machine
where she's adjusting soft cloth
and putting final touches to a tiny gown.
Her bentwood chair's a refuge
though her back negotiates
the time she'll be spending there.
Behind her, the rhythm of the house,
the chores to be done,
and out in the studio her husband
at his easel, a vision in his hand.
The children have faded into the garden.
She hears them whooping
and calling and holidaying.
The baby will be coming soon.

# For Moses

I've woven a rush basket
all soft and kind within.
Far adrift on the river,
parting the morning waters,
you'll sleep the hours away,
warmed by a milky sky.

I've woven a rush basket,
all soft and kind within,
save at one end the thorn
I've fixed will prick
when you awake, so the more
you stir the more you'll cry.

I've woven a rush basket
all soft and kind within.
Surely some woman will hear,
send help to fetch you in.
She'll embrace and keep you,
other people passing by.

# Blue Crystal Beads

after Rupert Bunny's painting *Madge Currie*, 1911

She had chosen a good dress,
a pink voile sash,
a matching ribbon for her hair
and she'd polished
her second-best walking shoes
until they shone
and while she was aware
they didn't match her gown
she wore the blue crystal beads
since people used to say
the beads brought out
the sonsy spirit in her eyes
and although her excuse
was that she'd sit sketching
at one with the mist and the sea
she sat waiting for him
and because of his promise
when she might have guessed
or perhaps she even knew
that he wouldn't come.

# The Wedding Ring

Matron held out a cardboard box
and opened it to show
a treasure trove of rings,
an accumulation of wedding bands
and each one dull and worn quite thin.
No rich pickings here,
no flashy stash of gold,
just a cache of personal effects,
a collection of articles lost and found.
But I recognised the wide gold band
worn by that warm-hearted soul
and knew the initials inscribed inside:
*CDB – EAB* and a wedding date in 1925.
A record of a marriage, a witness of sorrow,
it held two people together like a vice
that tightened as the years went by.
In the grey silence of the room
I retrieved the ring,
that modest token fraught with meaning
and satisfied I took it home.
I polished it until it shone,
a final thanks for all she'd done
and for her kindness.

# A Snatch of Memory

She was in her eighties then. And I was thirteen.
Now eighty, I've retrieved that memory of hers
and hold it as I would my own.
When young, she'd climb her front gate
and wait to see, as in a fairy tale or fantasy,
two Chinamen running into the morning.
Linked by a length of springy bamboo
that bounced to the rhythm of their jogging,
they kept their eyes to the road,
paying no heed to her friendly call.
They were making for the markets
and swinging from the pole, cane baskets of produce,
leeks and peppers, marrows and carrots,
mysterious little packets, bunches of green.

A marvel that she could recall that image,
that I could connect with it too –
a pair of figures on Walkerville Terrace,
conspicuous in conical hats of straw,
each in pale trousers and matching shirt
caught at the waist with a twisted cord.
Their heads were bent, their faces hidden,
their dark pigtails were flicking from side to side.

# Glass

*A glass*, she repeated with a smile.
As I waited for her to tell me
where to find that everyday object,
a thing of utility and mundane appeal,
I realised that the meaning of this common word
had absconded, had cut and run.
Standing in the kitchen she'd known
for over fifty years, she'd lost her bearings,
had lost knowledge of words and their meanings
and all the working days we'd shared.
Yes, some water was what was needed
but as time slipped by I stood there waiting.
I pointed to the yellow cupboards
but a wry grimace was her sole response.
So I found a glass, filled it at the tap
and she drank greedily and fast.
She took a deep breath
and retrieved the words *thank you*.
Then drawn to her past,
or still mindful of manners,
she thought to lift her right hand
and to wipe dry each side of her mouth.

# Baby and Shawl

after Gustav Klimt's painting *Baby*, 1917–1918

A profusion of colours cobbled together –
swirls of purple, a snatch of blue and snippets of red,
darker tones and two patches of yellow.
Leaping and looping, patterns mingle and tangle,
spring from the canvas in a maze of colour.
On first seeing the painting, minutes pass
before you glance up to discover
at very the top – a baby's face,
its head haloed with a white lace pillow.

You may think the child is belittled
by the busy bedding and the motley shawl.
Surely the artist contrived the setting
as a foil for innocence and grace.
But the infant he depicted is knowing,
has a presence, is at home in the world.
Its gaze is unwavering and its spirit soars
over the workaday domain.
Now at the end of the Great War
the artist has foreseen a future
where this baby will need resilience and power.

# Patchwork Blanket

You've walked away from your knitted blanket
with its squares of red and grey and green
on the pavement against a shop front
on the corner of Market Street and Castlereagh.
But you'll be back when evening
with its memories comes hustling in.
Just how much trust is needed
to leave your things unguarded,
to know that other homeless folk
won't souvenir your stuff?
To be sure that people passing
won't trample on your things?
There's some comfort in the fact
that the stream of shoppers veers aside
to avoid what looks like rubbish –
a muddled mosaic of a paperback,
a parcel tied with string,
some shabby underwear
and a rank pillow of striped ticking
huddled against the tiled steps
by this hang-out that's your home.
Even so, it's fair to say that when
you take up your bedding and mosey on
no one will think to ask where you have gone.

# See My Feathered Fingers

Someone said, *If my body were a temple*
*you'd decorate the walls.*
My body is my temple, my dwelling place,
my skin's the canvas that stories me.
See the bleeding heart and crucifix here?
It's for my mum when I began.
This knife is twisting for my dad, the time
I did him in – a bit of luck, that,
which explains the horseshoe on my arm.
The book and candle's a clever thing.
The dragon stretching down my back
in crimson and black and gold,
its claws embedded in my skin,
cost me more than I can say.
With my tattoos I've come this far
to free myself, to belong.
There's lighter stuff as well.
See my feathered fingers, rainbow bum
and the snake down there's a nice surprise.
All my life is here and where I've been,
what I've become. Now you see me
as I am, enter my temple,
come right in. Kiss my painted lips,
feel my studded tongue.

## Scar

What shocked us most was the scar.
It knifed across his forehead,
leapt over one eye and slashed his left cheek.
He relished his role at the story's centre.
We thrilled to his story of the terrible event –
the great train crash at night,
and how in an instant he was sent flying,
launched through a window, his body convulsing.
Then, the ambulances and his medical team,
the injured and the dead in the misty field,
the screams and groans and living confusion.
As the years passed we grew to admire him,
came to terms with his foibles, his ambiguities,
his recklessness and infidelities.
The scar that so marked him had faded
or seemed less livid in our eyes
yet his memory of the event
had strengthened, as had the shape
of the sounds that scarred his dreams.

# Cleaning Out the House

I balance at the top of my ladder and lean
into the cupboard to reach for the object there –
a single glass dish, unwanted or forgotten
and surprised by its weight I fetch it down,
setting it on the table with the cleaning things,
wondering at the purplish tinge it's taken on.
A single thought makes me press my thumb
against the first finger of my right hand.
I click my finger and let it fly
and the bowl gives voice to a crystal song,
resounding, continuing, widening.
I tap again, so that the chimes echo and sing,
to die away in a gentle thrum.
I wash and brush the facets clean,
put the bowl on the windowsill where the sun lends
living lights to a lattice design
which rises to form deep festoons
of flowers – chrysanthemums – around the rim.
As I work, my connection to the house,
the dank passageway, the sepia portraits,
the bleak days of dust and damp, fill my thoughts
and slowly clear as if with crystal clarity.

# The Porcelain Bowls

after Céleste Boursier-Mougerot's installation *clinamen*, 2013

From the gallery ahead comes an unbroken sound:
a resonant, tinkling and piping song.
Here, there's a round, blue artificial pond
and driven by a steady current,
a bevy of pure white bowls
is skimming over the stretch of water.
In the jostling confusion on the other side
they bob and veer, nudge each other and divide,
each curving back to the starting point
where, the water rippling,
they skitter away again, scattering, circulating.
Endlessly colliding, the bowls touch and recoil,
touch and spring away and all the time
clear and constant chimes ring out
to create a peal of bells.
A measure of this magic lies in the silence
of the people standing by. Even the children are still.
Bunched together, they sit or kneel,
or crouch on the floor, bottoms in the air.
They are mute, entranced,
tamed by the melody of the floating bowls.
Here's a fusion of music and movement and art,
a pretty dissonance, as the random tones
of this carillon are magnified
and reach out, echoing and re-echoing,
rising to sweep around and fill the room.

## Connections

Collection of the Art Gallery of South Australia, Mona Hatoum, *Traffic*, 2002

In this installation nothing seems untoward.
Two suitcases are standing side by side:
the grey commonplace, the green well-travelled.
You think of old stuff, long forgotten.
You imagine people on holiday
or those who disappear without a trace.
Or again, those with few possessions,
part of the great migrations across the world.
But stepping closer you're startled to discover,
breaking out from each case,
exposed, entangling and intermingling
as if to escape together, a spill of human hair.
There's a sense the hair is reaching out,
ready to bear witness, willing to testify.
And what of those travellers
whose lives and fate you try to imagine?
You'd call after them, release them
from their night's journey,
connect with them, save them if you could.
As you step back and walk away
you know you'll return,
the scene playing out in your mind,
a recurring, unnerving dream.

# III

# That Far Landscape

# Baggage

Collection of the Ellis Island Immigration Museum, New York

These cases have done with travelling.
Stacked high, they're nicely balanced,
the heft and haul of them forming an island,
an installation devised for tourists
and in an ordered confusion to catch the eye.
Here's a carpetbag made from a kelim
from Persia, possibly Kurdistan,
its frayed fabric woven in a geometric design.
Consider these trunks, the labels in tatters,
this stack of boxes, these chests, these crates,
these bags and satchels and cardboard cartons
and all those parcels tethered with cord.
This lidded basket has survived the voyage
like similar containers of wicker or cane,
all secured with a fretwork of string.

Imagine the babble of voices, the shouting,
and the utter confusion in this hall years ago
when the immigrants, baggage in tow,
set off alone or in groups and journeyed on,
making for a future largely unknown.
Then finally, no longer weighed down,
they flung wide their luggage, grasped
much-loved items, set their tables for rejoicing.
They opened their minds, their lives expanding,
and willed themselves to belong.

# Birch Broom

A broom was sweeping steadily back
and forth, toiling over those leaves amassing
in their thousands along the footpath
and gutters near the British Library.
Our eyes met. I smiled at him
and his wide brown face opened and shone.
*I been working here all the week lady*
*and you're the first person give me a smile.*
He set the broom straight, hands resting.
I felt a mixture of pleasure and shame.
I work with words, not leaves,
but can collect none
to match or to answer his simple truth.
I continued on my bookish way
and the street seemed desolate and long.
Over the years the broom
with its orderly rhythm returns
to my thoughts as it labours on.
And words like leaves keep mounting,
waiting for me to gather them.

## The Tablet

Collection of the State Library of South Australia, clay tablet,
c.2600–600 BCE, Ur, Mesopotamia

The proclamation's meaning is plain
so the man leans into his task,
setting down the command of his king,
Nebuchadnezzar, the powerful one.
He's aware there's no place for an error.
He works across the tablet's base,
pricking through the damp skin of clay,
his stylus pressing lightly, then more heavily,
until the job is done.

In the quiet workshop the hours stretch by,
light reaching through the slatted roof
to throw lengthening patterns over the sandy floor.
Outside, heat has baked the completed tablets,
the words becoming clearer under the sun

And the reward for all this toil –
a cowhide wallet with its jingle of coins.
He would buy sandals for his son,
tall now and ready for the trade.
He considers the young man, eyes measured,
back bent, just like his own.
The time has come for his dark hair to be tied
neatly at the nape of his neck.
Already he can shape a reed into the wedge
he needs and engrave his name. In turn
he will pass those skills to his son.

# Quipu

Collection of the Museum of the American Indian, Washington, DC

It's possible someone may unravel the mystery,
the riddle encoded in these cotton cords,
cords of varying lengths
and each knotted in a complex way,
then threaded again to a connecting cord.
The strings are dyed in natural colours,
the colours of rock and sky and cloud,
of forest foliage or the brown
and cream of grain and corn.

Who tied these knots?
Whose hands carried the messages
of the Incas; their poems or prayers,
recordings of events or news of the day?
All these were conveyed to the people
tethered along the great Incan road
strung across the networks of the empire.

Time may untie these knots, research reveal
knowledge of an alliance struck
or of a great sickness in the land.
Or even a plea that the road
be maintained in a better state
or taxes paid at once and without delay.

# Featherwork

after a pre-Colombian feathered panel, Peru

Let me show you a feathered panel
that radiates an energy,
its mystery drawn from the past.
A press of very small feathers,
yellow on the upper panel
and blue beneath,
is closely sewn,
tethered in layers and slanted
by a skilled craftsman
to intensify the natural sheen.
The panel was rolled for storage,
placed in a pottery jar and hidden
in sand at a time of danger.
And yet the colours are so vibrant
there's a glow
about them even today.
I would gladly put out my hand
to stroke this tender pelt
but it rests in a showcase,
secure beneath glass
in a busy studio where tourists
stand gazing, gazing in silence
at beauty uncompromised.

# The Sound of Jade Earrings

When at last showers fell, the Mayan people danced.
Men danced, arms high over their heads,
and woman danced, throwing off their heavy loads.
Skipping children placed fruit and flowers
in thanks at the feet of the great Creator.

Far above, priests gathered on the parapet
that cut a swathe across the pyramid.
Standing aside, one of them sought answers.
He felt alone in the world.
He despised the ceremony and ritual,
stared at the great vault of the sky,
clearer than ever now and far away.
His thoughts turned to the legends,
to the sayings of the old people.
He doubted more rain would come.
He had no trust in the rain god Chaac
whose waters, spent in shallow pools,
were never enough to feed the maize.
Breathing in incense and the rank smell
of sacrificial blood he turned aside,
questions like serpents tangling in his mind.

A dry wind knifed through his headdress,
the red and gold and emerald feathers fluttering,
then caught at his jade earrings, set the stones rattling,
and even as he heard rejoicing from the plaza,
the voices rising to where he stood,
that small sound unaccountably filled him with dread.

# Sepik Mask

Collection of the South Australian Museum

Pinned high on a wall the mask stares ahead
as if a living presence and alert.
Two closely woven ovals of reed or grass
are laced together in a geometric design,
this wickerwork rounding out to form a face.
The spine-like nose sits firm and strong
with two shells attached as ornament.
Likewise, cowrie shells are fixed as ears.
Two hollows, dark and close, suggest the eyes:
eyes that stare into the cramped brown room
and grieve for the past, mourn the absence
of shrill bird calls, the splash of parrots,
lush greenery and rain sheeting down.
The mask is daubed with ochre and clay,
chipped and weathered and faded over time.
In the homeland the glad yam harvest
has finally been gathered,
the people singing and dancing,
shrieking children joining the throng.
Here in an alien place the spirits
who dwelt within the mask have fled
and now are scattered and dispossessed.

# Tang Figurine

Collection of the Shanghai Museum, China

Secure in her place in the museum
she's amongst others of her kind.
Perhaps she recalls details of her life,
how she was shaped, trimmed down
and put through fire.
She was to follow her mistress
into the tomb; instead, she stands erect.
No longer young, she has come through.
Her hands, hidden beneath ample sleeves,
are clasped across her breast.
Although there's a russet tinge to her gown
her colours are faded, her face worn.
There's a calm about her, a serenity,
and playing across her face, confident
yet a little hesitant, her lips just lifting,
the beginnings of a smile.
There's understanding, acceptance
and she is appropriately proud:
enough that she has survived.

# Nails

after Frida Kahlo's oil painting *La Columna Rota*, 1944

The stone column that's become your spine
is black and bloodstained. It's fractured too
and offers slight support.
But the steel brace is obdurate,
grasping you in a surgical embrace,
encircling you and keeping you straight.
Here you've pictured your naked torso,
arms and head and face
perforated by nails like tacks,
the soft flesh taking them in.
These may represent petty grievances
or pricks of anxiety and doubt.
But the largest nail has punctured your heart,
that part of your body most betrayed.
Like petals slipping down your cheeks
small scattered tears reveal the pain.
You've fashioned your lone eyebrow
into the dark shape of a bird,
alerting us to the rasp of its flight.
It would wing its way to freedom,
to that far landscape,
but you have placed yourself
against a bleak and fissured terrain
reflecting the grief and longing
that overshadowed your singular life.

# The Bronze Hand

Collection of the British Museum, bronze, Arabia, 100–300 CE

This hand has come to represent a man.
It is clearly the work of an artisan.
The fingers are sturdy, squat and firm,
the knuckles thickened,
the nails spoon-shaped and worn.
There's the forceful thumb
and the little finger that veers sideways,
possibly broken at some point in time.
An inscription in a Semitic tongue
is ingeniously spaced, reaching out
to span the back of the hand.
It asks the god Ta'lab Ruyam
for good fortune and well-being.
You move on but that hand beckons,
drawing you back to the glass case
where the years contract and slip away.
You stand there and reconsider
a life once lived and continuing,
as the artist also stood
and surveyed the piece he'd wrought,
surely content with what he'd done.

# The Turban

I thought of you again today and the way,
as an older man, you sat straight and tall and bearded,
alone on a wooden bench in the mall.

You were well dressed but stood out for
the twisted length of cotton, meticulously folded,
that formed the covering for your head.

As you watched the passers-by did you observe
a drabness that made you yearn for your homeland
and the crescendo of colours there?

You were part of our urban life
yet seemingly apart, as if piecing things together
and waiting for wisdom to come.

And I could have bent and spoken to you
but it would have seemed an impertinence,
an intrusion. It was unnecessary.

Now years later I am writing in celebration
to say you're not forgotten. I took delight
in your composure. And your bright purple turban.

# In Afghanistan

after Elyas Alavi's video *We Die So That*, 2017

If death comes without warning, haphazardly,
in the cemetery at least there is order
and symmetry in the long rows of graves
hacked out of the leaden earth,
stone resounding against stone
where birds are loitering
to snap up a worm or two.

On a hill and tied to a bamboo pole
a flag's flimsy remnants rise and fall.
Time has given it a whipping,
stripping away the green band of prosperity,
the red of royalty
colours trailing away in shreds,
the fraying ends of an era.
Which leaves the black, a relic
from the past flying in tatters,
the flag reconfigured, redefined
by the scissoring thrust of the wind.

From the past the sound
not of an anthem but of street music,
of people dancing, dancing the *attan*
and taking joy in its symmetry.
People are stepping into the patterns,
these repeated rhythms that have united them;
a certainty handed down from the past,
the music of the *rubab* and the drum
bringing them together and playing on.

## In the Ukraine

On TV news last night,
a winding road,
a tank speeding by
with the dust rising
to camouflage
a single sunflower
tilted towards the sky.

## Field Flowers

after the work of the German artist Otto Dix

The soldier put his machine gun aside.
Turning artist he would sit and sketch
the craters and the broken earth
where dandelions and daisies,
those pretty unpretentious flowers
that heralded Spring and new life,
grew and flourished
among the pungent odours
and scenes of horror and death
that caught and held him hard
and fettered him for life.

# The Floating Islands

Hoi An, Vietnam

Guidebook open and coffee at hand,
I'm enjoying the lazy morning
when a movement catches my eye.
I turn and watch in wonder
as along the Thu Bon river
tiny grass-green islands
come floating serenely
and mysteriously by.
Breaking away from the river bank
and carried on a steady current
this fleet of islands has set sail
through tawny morning mist
for the coast, there to slip
unnoticed into the darker green
and everlasting tumult of the sea.

# The Finger

Collection of the War Remnants Museum, Ho Chi Minh City, Vietnam

On the second floor the photos arc
and flare their message from the war.
In this image the finger is slender,
elegant and not deformed.
The nail is perfect, neatly clipped.
And yet the finger stands alone,
just this one finger,
extending from the boy's left hand,
then to become one with the wrist
in an immense bulbous mass of flesh.

So, the boy was born during the war,
after the low-flying plane had trailed
its sickly mist over the town
and across the terraced valley,
and he must manage as best he can.
Maybe he will trim and tidy,
sort out and sequence,
make use of this wartime remnant.
Maybe he will keep it under his jacket
when the tourists come by.

# The Citadel

Hue, Vietnam

Here at Emperor Gia Long's citadel
the enclosing walls still stand
but in this inconspicuous spot
the bricks have split apart,
a crack revealing tightly packed soil
where you find a knot of greenery
drawn to the sun,
straining, cascading out –
bright lean grasses,
the thick dry fronds,
some lush fern, heart-shaped,
and leaves neat as a nettle.
A loamy fragrance is rising
from this tranquil place
and insects, those survivors,
are gathering, darting around.

# Bamboo

There's a surge
through the great bamboo
as rallied by the wind
the timbers strain
then splash the sky,
the tallest rampant,
like a warlord's pennant,
seething and tossing,
ominous as a prophesy.

And when the winds
fall away
fronds break free,
others rustle,
whisper together,
fall silent and still
as if a proclamation
previously heard
is only now understood
for all that it might signify.

# Riding the Ocean

after Hokusai's *The Great Wave off Kanagawa* from *The Thirty-six Views of Mt Fuji*, 1830–34

You never tire of this image,
the one where three boats ride the ocean
and the fishermen bend low
hunkering in their craft,
the sea rising around them.
Ahead, a single wave,
a towering mass of deepest blue,
rears up and from its height
tosses off white droplets of foam
that drift across a sombre sky.
See how readily, how mysteriously,
they become small flakes of snow
falling on the immortal mountain,
far, far Mount Fuji,
as it contemplates the countryside.
And when in time the melting snow
flows back across the land
to join the ocean again
the fishermen still trawl,
their boats embracing them
and the sea rising.

# Caught In the Weather

after Hokusai's *Ejiri in Suruga Province* from *The Thirty-six Views of Mt Fuji*, 1830–34

Seven travellers are caught in a storm.
One, a woman, seems to be journeying alone.

The pamphlets she was to deliver have fallen
from her kimono; oblivious, she struggles on.

The men clutch their flip-flapping clothing
and lean into the gale; they too are battling.

One of them has let go his hat. It's been blown
high into the sky where the artist has it join

the flying papers and now, the leaves torn
from trees bent sideways under the strain.

Leaves, hat and papers hover for a time,
riding the air with a mind of their own.

The storm will pass and in the calm
these sturdy folk will journey easily again.

Away in the mist Mount Fuji stands benign;
a mythic presence within this small frame.

# Burial of St Catherine of Alexandria

after the painting by Rupert Bunny, c.1896

See how the rosy shades of morning
have given light to a drab landscape
or perhaps the glow of evening
is spreading warmth over the scene.

Their unrehearsed hands clenched tight
against the pale winding sheet,
their bare feet just leaving the earth,
four angels are lifting their small burden.
Their robes are woven in colours of grief.

See how these young angels hover,
their wings upthrust, upbeat,
rising to slip away as steadily
and smoothly as a swelling song,
the heavens drawing them in.

Catherine, freed from her frailty,
from the horrors of human savagery,
awaits the promise of a resting place.
See her tender halo, her face at peace.

# The Merry Cemetery

Sapanta, Romania

The day is fresh and clear and blue-skied
but that colour is not so deep
as the Sapanta blue of the wooden memorials
atop these tranquil graves.

Over every cross a peaked gable is set
to prevent weathering and to protect
small portraits of the dead,
glossy now after the recent rain.
There are poems about their personalities,
while on each frame a rustic design
patterned with birds and flowers.
Beneath these deep blue markers lie
local farmers, a butcher, and Ion the policeman.
Andru is pictured as he fell from his tractor
and Dimitru, well-known about town,
is shown with brandy bottle in hand.
Solemn Heldis Ioanis displays
a hammer and sickle insignia with pride.
Irini and Angelika and Catina
although now at rest, seem content
and will be remembered
for their spinning, weaving and gardening.
Here's little Maria in a dainty dress,
struck by a car when only six.

An angel bent over a lyre,
a sorrowing figure lost in thought,
an imposing statue in granite,

could never upstage the novel charm
and happy disorder of this vibrant place,
its colour and its spontaneity.

Over every grave as if given life
from what lies beneath,
miniature gardens are flourishing,
now rain-soaked, shimmering.
A perfume hangs in the air,
close-by, transitory, unfamiliar.
As far as the eye can see,
ferns and spreading pink pentas,
wallflowers, drifts of yellow cosmos.
There are brilliant amaranthus,
clusters of love-in-a-mist,
a splash of scarlet salvias.
Unhurried, visitors quietly chatter
while scarcely noticed, fat little sparrows
flit from plot to plot.

www.ingramcontent.com/pod-product-compliance
Lightning Source LLC
Chambersburg PA
CBHW062141100526
44589CB00014B/1643